Keeping warm and cool

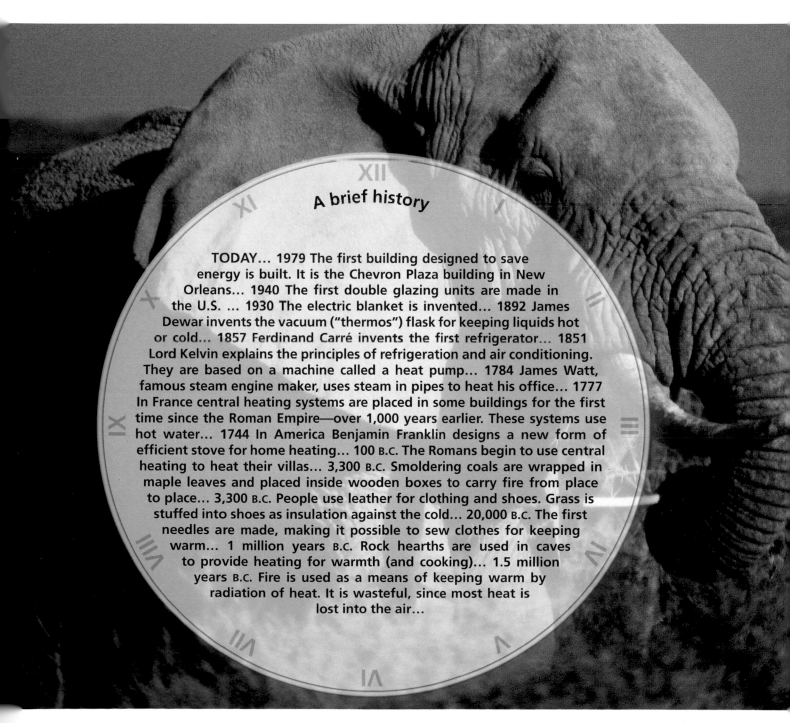

A brief history

TODAY... 1979 The first building designed to save energy is built. It is the Chevron Plaza building in New Orleans... 1940 The first double glazing units are made in the U.S. ... 1930 The electric blanket is invented... 1892 James Dewar invents the vacuum ("thermos") flask for keeping liquids hot or cold... 1857 Ferdinand Carré invents the first refrigerator... 1851 Lord Kelvin explains the principles of refrigeration and air conditioning. They are based on a machine called a heat pump... 1784 James Watt, famous steam engine maker, uses steam in pipes to heat his office... 1777 In France central heating systems are placed in some buildings for the first time since the Roman Empire—over 1,000 years earlier. These systems use hot water... 1744 In America Benjamin Franklin designs a new form of efficient stove for home heating... 100 B.C. The Romans begin to use central heating to heat their villas... 3,300 B.C. Smoldering coals are wrapped in maple leaves and placed inside wooden boxes to carry fire from place to place... 3,300 B.C. People use leather for clothing and shoes. Grass is stuffed into shoes as insulation against the cold... 20,000 B.C. The first needles are made, making it possible to sew clothes for keeping warm... 1 million years B.C. Rock hearths are used in caves to provide heating for warmth (and cooking)... 1.5 million years B.C. Fire is used as a means of keeping warm by radiation of heat. It is wasteful, since most heat is lost into the air...

Dr. Brian Knapp

Word list

These are some science words that you should look out for as you go through the book. They are shown using CAPITAL letters.

CELSIUS SCALE
A scale for measuring temperature named for its inventor, scientist Anders Celsius. On this scale there are 100 divisions, called degrees, between 0 (the temperature of melting ice) and 100 (the temperature of boiling water).

COLD-BLOODED
A term used for animals that do not maintain a constant body temperature and need to get heat from their surroundings before they can become active.

CONDUCTION
The flow of heat from warm to cool objects when they are touching or from a warm part of an object to cooler parts of the same object.

CONDUCTOR
A substance that allows heat to flow through it easily. Good heat conductors are also usually good conductors of electricity.

CONVECTION
The churning movement that happens in liquids and gases when they are heated from below.

CORK
A natural bark of the cork oak tree. It is a very good insulator.

DOUBLE GLAZING
Two panes of glass used in a window to trap air and improve insulation.

DRAFT
A flow of cold air in a home.

EVAPORATE
To change from liquid water to water vapor in the air.

FIBER
Long strands of material. Hair, fur, and wool are natural fibers, but many artificial fibers are also commonly used.

GOOSEBUMPS
The little pimples of skin that stick up when your skin is cold.

HEAT
A form of energy. Heat is produced when work is done, such as moving around. The fast flow of electricity in a wire can also produce heat, as can burning a substance like gas.

HYPOTHERMIA
A serious condition caused when the inside of the body becomes very cold.

INSULATOR
A substance that will not conduct heat very well. Good heat insulators are usually also good insulators of electricity.

PLASTIC
A solid material made from oil.

RADIATION
The direct transfer of heat between objects by means of heat rays.

SHIVER
To shake uncontrollably due to cold.

SWEAT
To lose large amounts of water and salts from the pores in the skin.

TEMPERATURE
A measure of how warm or cool something is.

THERMOMETER
An instrument for measuring temperature.

VACUUM FLASK
A flask designed to keep its contents hot or cold for long periods by stopping conduction, convection, and radiation of heat.

WARM-BLOODED
A term used for animals that maintain a constant temperature inside their bodies and do not depend on the temperature of their surroundings.

WEAVE, WOVEN
To make a fine net of fibers for use in clothing.

Contents

Feeling warmth

Although we can sense hot and cold in a general way, our bodies are not very good at measuring it.

People often say how warm it is outside, or how warm or cold something is.

When we describe something as warm or cold, we are comparing it to what feels hotter or colder than us.

1

Heat flows from the hot Sun to our colder body. As more heat is transferred, we can feel uncomfortably hot. That is when people on beaches head for the sea to cool off.

2

In the sea heat flows from our warm body to the colder water. After a while we are cool and go back on the beach.

3

The Sun now warms us up again.

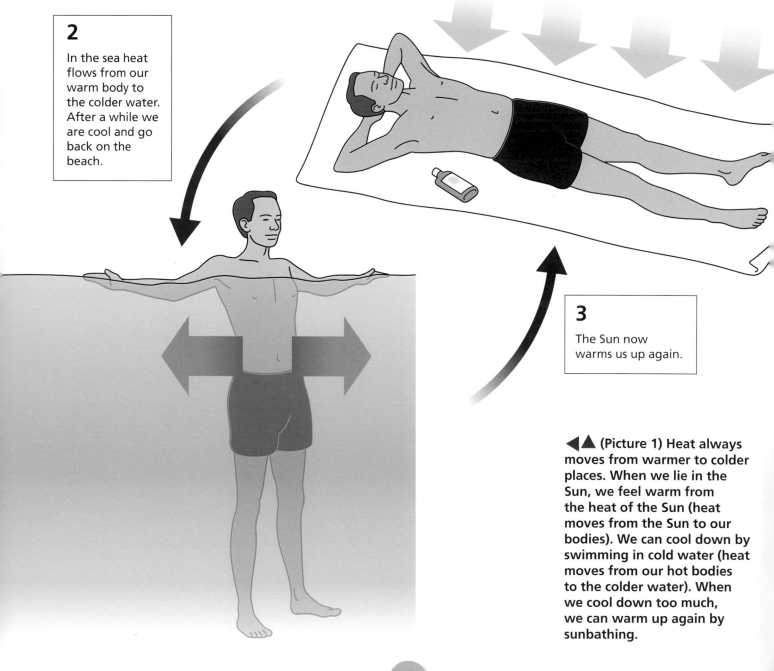

◄▲ (Picture 1) Heat always moves from warmer to colder places. When we lie in the Sun, we feel warm from the heat of the Sun (heat moves from the Sun to our bodies). We can cool down by swimming in cold water (heat moves from our hot bodies to the colder water). When we cool down too much, we can warm up again by sunbathing.

Heat flows from warm to cold

HEAT always flows from a warm place to a colder one (Picture 1). For example, the heat from the Sun can be so strong in summer that we get too hot. That is why we then try to cool down by going into the cool shade or taking a swim in cool water. We cool down because our bodies are losing heat to their surroundings—the shade or the water.

If we go outside in winter, our warm bodies lose heat to the cold air. Because we are now losing heat faster than our bodies can replace it, we feel cold. At this time of year to try to stop losing too much heat, we have to put on warm clothing.

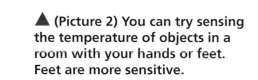

Wood

Metal

▲ (Picture 2) You can try sensing the temperature of objects in a room with your hands or feet. Feet are more sensitive.

Feeling warm and cold

Our feeling of warmness—called TEMPERATURE—is actually quite unreliable and easily fooled.

Feet are among the most temperature-sensitive parts of the body. Even so, if you put one bare foot on a piece of wood and put the other bare foot on a sheet of metal, the metal will feel colder, even though you know the wood and the metal are at the same temperature (Picture 2).

Metals feel colder than other materials even when they are in the same surroundings and at the same temperature. That is because they carry heat away from the feet or hands quickly. You will find out more about this way of sharing heat on pages 8 and 9.

Summary
- We sense warm and cold through our skin, but not very accurately.
- Heat always flows from a warmer place to a colder place.

Measuring warmth

Thermometers are instruments for measuring the temperature of objects accurately.

We cannot tell the temperature reliably by touch, so we need a better way of measuring it. The instrument we use is called a **THERMOMETER** (Picture 1).

What is a thermometer?

A thermometer is usually a plastic or glass tube with a very narrow space, or bore, running through its length. The bottom of the tube is connected to a bulb that holds a liquid. Thermometers with red bulbs use a runny liquid called alcohol, while thermometers with silver bulbs use a runny metal called mercury.

Once some liquid has been put in the bulb, all the air is sucked out from the top of the tube, and the thermometer is sealed.

Warming the bulb causes both the liquid and the glass to swell (expand), but the liquid swells much

100°C—boiling point of water

0°C—freezing point of water

more than the glass does. The extra volume of liquid has nowhere else to go but up the tube. If the tube is narrow enough, the liquid will rise a long way up the tube and will be easy to see.

Temperature scale

Now that we have a sensitive way of measuring warmth, we need to draw a scale on the tube.

The scale we use is marked in units called degrees and is called the **CELSIUS SCALE** for the Swedish scientist Anders Celsius.

On this scale boiling water is 100°C (one hundred degrees Celsius), and freezing water is 0°C (zero degrees Celsius). Notice that we use a small circle as a shorthand for the word degree.

◀ **(Picture 1)** A thermometer is a narrow tube with a thin space inside and a bulb filled with liquid. As the liquid gets hotter, it swells in the bulb and rises up the tube. The scale on its side is marked in degrees Celsius.

Making measurements

It is important to become familiar with using a thermometer. If you are measuring the temperature of a solid object, you place the bulb of the thermometer so that it touches the object. If you are measuring a gas (such as air) or a liquid (such as water), you place the thermometer bulb in the gas or liquid.

▼ (Picture 2) It takes time for the thermometer to give a steady reading. You can test that by putting a thermometer in hot water and writing down the temperature every ten seconds. When a reading is the same as the one before it, the thermometer is giving an accurate reading.

You should only take readings from a thermometer after the liquid in it has had enough time to rise or fall. Always wait for the level of the liquid in the tube to become steady. That means you would normally wait a little while before making a reading (Picture 2).

Summary

- A thermometer is a device for measuring temperature.
- A thermometer takes a little while to react to a change in temperature.
- Thermometers use the Celsius scale.

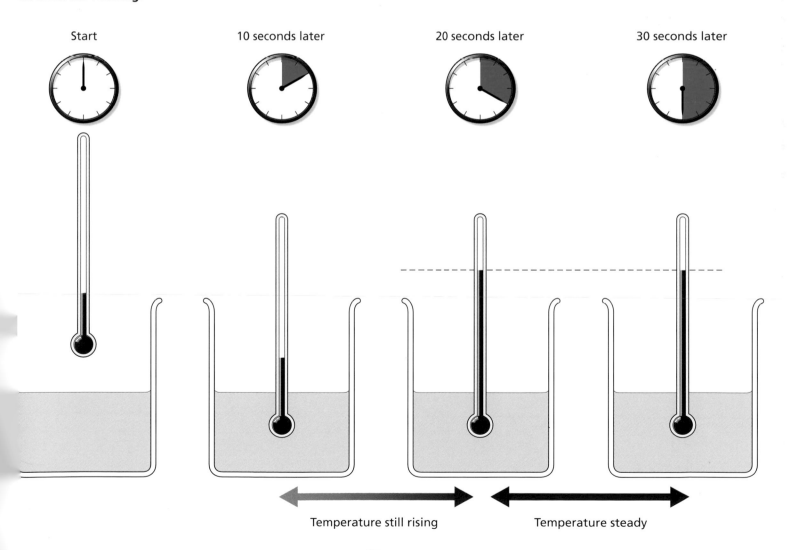

Start | 10 seconds later | 20 seconds later | 30 seconds later

Temperature still rising   Temperature steady

Conduction—traveling heat

Heat travels from hotter objects to colder ones. If the objects are touching, the way the heat moves is called CONDUCTION.

There are three ways that heat can travel. One way is shown here; the other two ways are described on pages 10 to 13.

Warmth by touching

If you placed a poker in a fire, the end in the fire would get hot because it would be touching the fiery coals (Picture 1). But after a few moments more and more of the poker would start to get hot until, if it were kept in the fire too long, the poker would be too hot to touch even at the end furthest from the fire.

Notice that the heat has traveled from the coals to the rod and then from the hot end of the rod to the cold end. You should remember that heat always travels this way—from hotter places to colder ones.

Conductors

Some things are very good at allowing heat to travel through them. They are called **CONDUCTORS**. Metals are very good conductors of heat, as you could tell from what happened to the poker in the fire.

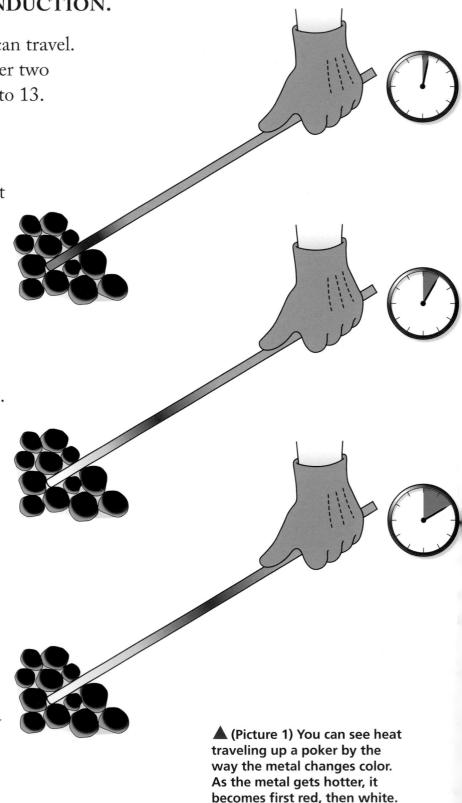

▲ **(Picture 1) You can see heat traveling up a poker by the way the metal changes color. As the metal gets hotter, it becomes first red, then white.**

The reason a metal object at room temperature feels cold to the touch is because the metal is conducting heat away from your skin.

Some metals, however, are even better conductors of heat than others (Picture 2). Copper is one of the best conductors, which is why it is used in high-quality cooking pans. Aluminum is cheaper and almost as good a conductor, so it is used in cheaper pans. Iron is not as good a conductor, so is less commonly used for pans.

Insulators

Things that conduct heat poorly are called **INSULATORS**. Nearly everything besides metal is a poor conductor—and therefore an insulator. For example, the air around us is an insulator, as is water.

One way to show that water is a poor conductor is to put a pan of water under a burner and heat it from above. It is easy to get the water to boil at the top of the pan while the water in the bottom stays cooler. You can even keep ice and boiling water near each other in the same tube for several minutes before the ice melts (Picture 3).

Skin is a poor conductor of heat. That is why, if you touch a hot object, you are likely to burn yourself: The heat cannot be carried away quickly, and so the surface of your skin gets hot enough to burn.

Note: Metals are usually good conductors of both heat and electricity.

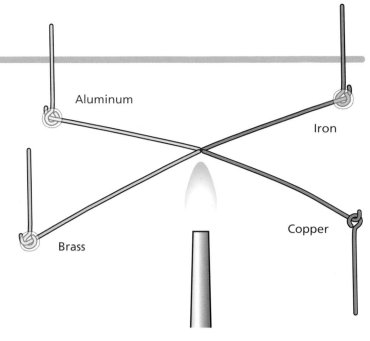

▲ (Picture 2) In this experiment copper, aluminum, iron, and brass hooks are attached to wires of the same metals with blobs of wax. When the wires are heated, the copper conducts heat best, and so the wax melts first, and the copper hook falls first.

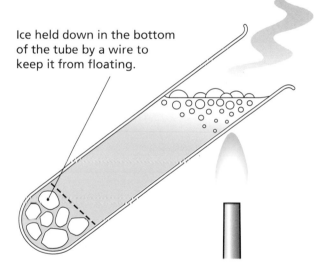

Ice held down in the bottom of the tube by a wire to keep it from floating.

▲ (Picture 3) Water conducts heat very slowly. In fact, you can boil water in the top of a tube without melting ice cubes at the bottom. (To find out why the water is heated from the top in this case, see convection, page 10.)

Summary

- Conduction is the flow of heat between two things that are touching.
- Heat travels from the hotter object to the colder one.
- Metals are the best conductors.
- Water and air are poor heat conductors and are called insulators.

Convection—rising heat

Heat makes liquids and gases expand and get lighter.
As a result, they rise. We call the rising heat CONVECTION.

Water and air are very poor conductors, but they still allow heat to travel very efficiently. How do they do this?

Rising heat

To understand why heat travels through gases and liquids like air and water, we first need to know that liquids and gases both flow easily. We also need to know that hot things weigh less than cold things—they get lighter as they warm up. These two properties explain how heat moves through air and water—it moves by something we call convection.

How convection works

Remember that in Picture 3 on page 9 we heated water from above. In that example the hot water stayed on top of the ice because it was lighter than the water below. But when water is heated from below, something very different happens (Picture 1). The water at the bottom gets lighter and rises up through the colder water, bobbing to the surface like a cork. At the same time, colder water sinks to the bottom and is heated in turn.

As you can see, the result is a natural churning, or overturning movement, that makes sure that the heat is spread evenly through the water.

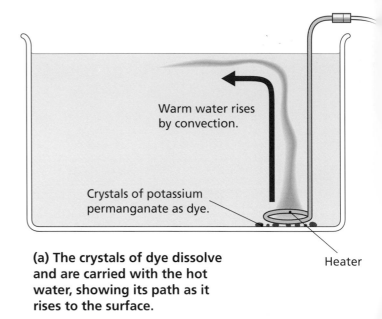

Warm water rises by convection.

Crystals of potassium permanganate as dye.

Heater

(a) The crystals of dye dissolve and are carried with the hot water, showing its path as it rises to the surface.

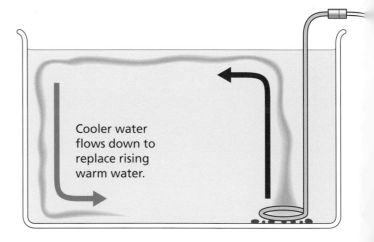

Cooler water flows down to replace rising warm water.

(b) The hot water on the surface cools and sinks on the opposite side of the tank, while more hot water rises.

▲ **(Picture 1) The way convection works is easily seen by using a dye to trace the flow of water. After a while the water in the tank becomes uniformly colored, showing how convection stirs up the water. For convection to work, the heater must be placed at the *bottom* of the tank.**

Convection heaters

A convection heater is a very effective way of heating air (Picture 2). It works like a chimney with an electric heater at the bottom. As the heater warms the air, the air gets lighter and rises up the "chimney" inside the heater. Cold air is then drawn in from below.

Using this method, warm air can be circulated around a room without using any fan or motor (Picture 3).

Heated air rises from the heating element and circulates around the room.

Cooler air taken in.

▲▶ (Picture 2) How a convection heater works.

Heated air rises from the heating element, passes out of the convection heater, and circulates around the room.

Cooler air taken in.

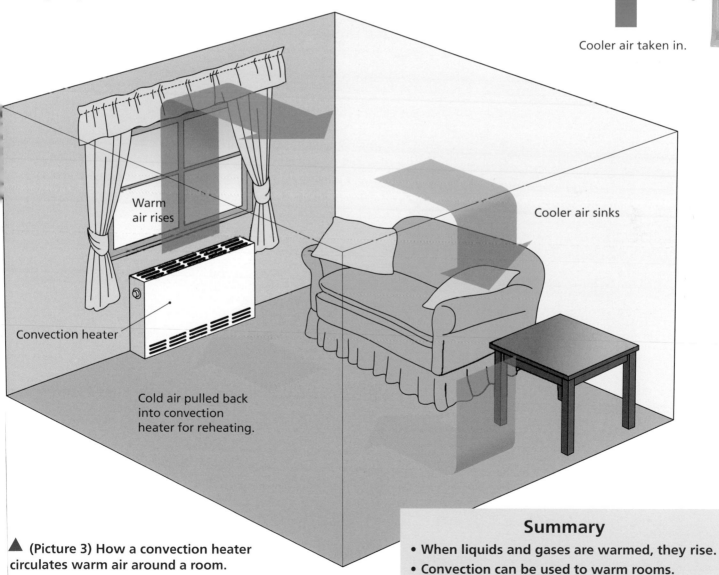

Warm air rises

Convection heater

Cold air pulled back into convection heater for reheating.

Cooler air sinks

▲ (Picture 3) How a convection heater circulates warm air around a room.

Summary
- When liquids and gases are warmed, they rise.
- Convection can be used to warm rooms.

Radiation—heat rays

Heat can be passed between objects that are not touching—even through the depths of space. This is called RADIATION.

Stand outside in the open, and feel the warmth of a summer's day on your face. Or stand in front of an open fire. You will immediately feel the warmth even though you are not touching the source of heat.

The fact that we can feel the warmth from the Sun, even though it is millions of kilometers away in space, shows that warmth can be transferred between things that are not touching, even when there is no air. This way of transferring heat is called radiation.

Rays of warmth

Everything—including ourselves—gives off heat rays. Hot things give off more heat than they soak up, and cold things soak up more heat than they give out.

You can think of rays of heat in the same way as rays of light. The only difference is that the rays of heat are invisible. Both heat and light rays travel in straight lines (Picture 1). That is why, if you stand in the shade, it feels cooler than when you stand in the sunshine; or why, when you stand in front of a fire, your front can get toasty warm while your back feels like ice (Picture 2).

Bouncing heat rays

Because heat rays are like light rays, you can bounce, or reflect, heat rays off a mirror or other shiny surface.

Dark surfaces soak up more heat than light ones. That can be shown with an instrument called a radiometer, which spins because each of its panels is painted black on one side and white on the other (Picture 3).

The difference in heat soaked up by dark and light surfaces explains

▶ (Picture 1) Heat rays are like light rays. They travel in straight lines and bounce off the walls of a room.

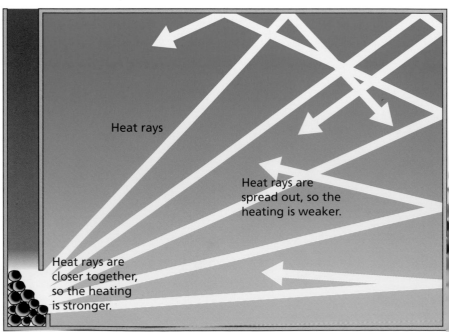

Heat rays

Heat rays are spread out, so the heating is weaker.

Heat rays are closer together, so the heating is stronger.

▲ (Picture 2) Places in the shadow of the heat are colder than those in the line of heat rays. Because heat travels in straight lines, just like light, you can use the light of a fire to show where the heat rays go.

Colder away from the source of heat.

Warmer region close to and directly in front of the fire.

why people tend to wear light-colored clothes in summer. The light color reflects away more heat than the dark color. The difference can be seen if you set up thermometers in black and white bottles and put them in direct sunshine (Picture 4).

Heating a room by radiation

Many rooms are heated by radiation. An open fire heats a room almost entirely by radiation, as you can see in Picture 2.

Room panels filled with warm water are called radiators because that is mainly how they work. (A panel radiator also uses convection to heat a room.)

Summary

- Heat rays travel in straight lines.
- Places in shadow are much colder than places facing a fire or radiator.
- Dark colors soak up heat better than light colors.

▼ (Picture 3) The panels in a radiometer spin because sunshine heats the dark side more than the light side.

▶ (Picture 4) A dark-colored bottle will soak up more of the Sun's heat than a light-colored bottle. That is why the thermometer in the dark bottle shows the higher temperature.

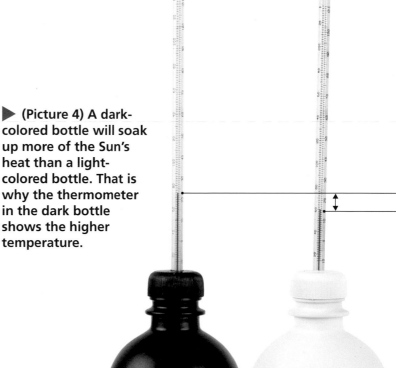

Keeping food and drinks warm

To keep food and drinks warm, we need to keep them away from cold air.

Now that we know there are three ways in which heat can travel—conduction, convection, and radiation—we can find ways of controlling how heat moves. This is vital if we want to keep things warm (or cool).

Insulating eggs

The bigger the difference in temperature between two objects, the faster the hotter one will lose heat. For example, warm food has a much higher temperature than the air in a room. As a result, it can lose heat rapidly.

If you pick up a hot boiled egg with a paper towel, for example, the heat will quickly move through the paper and make it too hot to hold. The egg will lose heat so fast that it will cool down very quickly.

To keep an egg hot, the egg needs to be insulated. The thicker the material, the more it insulates, so one simple solution is to make a cover thicker (Picture 1).

The stay-hot flask

Keeping drinks or food hot for long periods of time is difficult. The Scottish scientist Sir James Dewar was the inventor of the principle of the stay-hot flask we now call a **VACUUM FLASK**

(Picture 2). He set out to keep heat from being exchanged between the inside and outside of a flask. His answer was to make a glass bottle with two walls and then to suck all of the air out of the space between the walls. Heat could not pass by conduction through the empty space. Dewar then put a very thick **CORK** stopper in the top of the flask. Cork is a very good insulator, so little heat was lost through the opening. Because heat was not lost at the top, no convection occured.

Dewar then tackled the problem of radiation. He coated the glass with silver

▼(Picture 1) Insulating covers can be made of thick cloth, knitted wool, and other materials. The temperature difference between the inside and the outside can be checked with a thermometer.

so that any heat radiated would be bounced back.

In this way, by understanding how heat is transferred, Dewar was able to keep the contents of the flask warm (or cold) for many hours.

▼▶ (Picture 2) How a vacuum flask works.

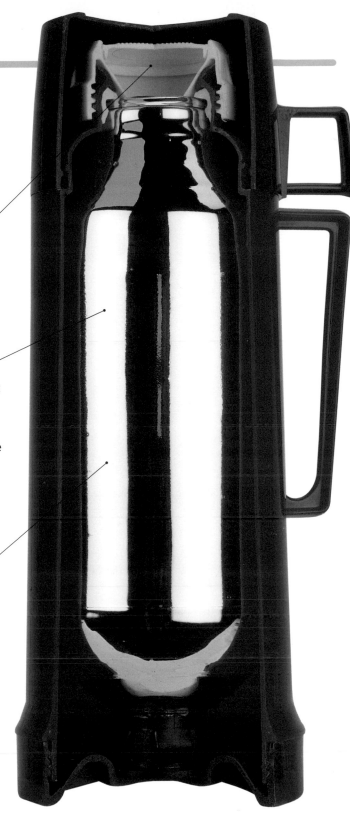

The stopper is made from insulating cork or plastic.

Glass is a strong material even when it is thin. It is easy to coat with silver and does not take up or give out flavors to the liquids it contains.

"Silvering" reflects radiated heat.

The space between the layers of glass is a vacuum, to prevent conduction.

Plastic or steel case protects the glass flask inside.

Summary

- Hot food and drinks lose heat by conduction, convection, and radiation.
- Increasing the insulation around them and adding a cover keeps food and drinks hot for longer.
- A vacuum flask slows radiation, convection, and conduction and keeps food and drinks hot for many hours.

Warm homes

To keep homes warm, we need to insulate places where warm air can leak out by conduction, convection or radiation.

Homes are boxes full of air (Picture 1). To keep a home warm, we heat the air. As a result, we don't want to lose too much warm air. But at the same time, we need to let some air escape, or the air will become stale and unhealthy.

Walls

The walls of a house may be made of stone, wood, or brick.

Brick and stone conduct heat away quickly, so they may let some heat escape. Wood conducts less heat, and so the walls feel warmer.

We don't want to lose more heat through the walls than we need to, so we want to build walls out of a good insulator. In most cases insulating sheets are placed between the inner wall and the outer wall. This traps air and stops convection and conduction.

The inside of the insulation is lined with a thin sheet of aluminum. It reflects any heat radiated from the inner wall back into the home.

Roofs

Hot air rises, and so the hottest part of any room is the air near the ceiling. For houses with several floors the lower floors can be used as a kind of underfloor heating for the rooms above. So we don't need insulation between the floors of a house. But the upper ceiling can lose a lot of heat to the roof, so that is where we need to put insulation. Most lofts are insulated with fiberglass or pellets of a foamy material.

Windows

Glass is not as good an insulator as brick, so much of the heat in a room can be lost through the windows. But if we can keep air from circulating past the window, we can reduce the loss quite a bit. **DOUBLE GLAZING** traps a layer of air between two panes of glass, making an invisible insulating layer.

Doors

By opening and closing doors, we automatically let in some fresh air and let some hot air get away. That is a good way to get fresh air into a house. The only time it is a problem is if there are **DRAFTS**, coming in under the door, for example, so that the air escapes too quickly.

Summary
- To keep heating bills as low as possible, homes need to be insulated.
- Walls and lofts are insulated with fiberglass, foam, and other insulating materials.
- Windows can be insulated with double glazing.

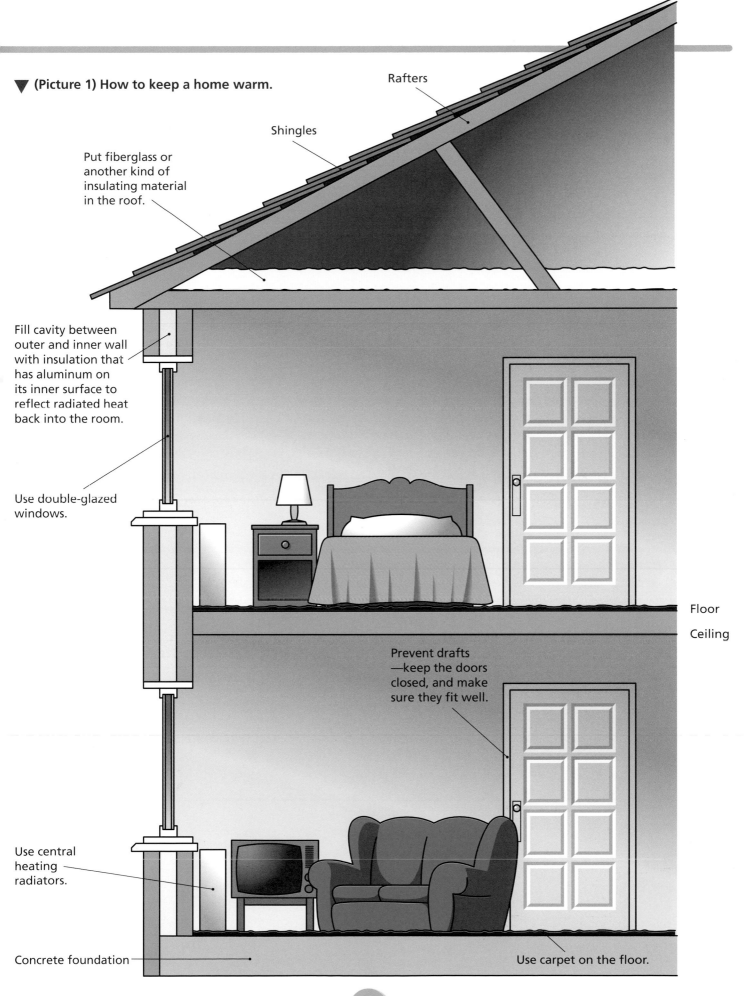

▼ (Picture 1) How to keep a home warm.

Rafters

Shingles

Put fiberglass or another kind of insulating material in the roof.

Fill cavity between outer and inner wall with insulation that has aluminum on its inner surface to reflect radiated heat back into the room.

Use double-glazed windows.

Floor

Ceiling

Prevent drafts —keep the doors closed, and make sure they fit well.

Use central heating radiators.

Concrete foundation

Use carpet on the floor.

How our bodies keep warm

We need to keep at just the right level of warmth. To achieve this, our bodies have ways of controlling how warm we are.

People, and all other living things, spend much of their time keeping warm. That is because the bodies of all living things need to be within a narrow temperature range in order to work well. For humans the normal body temperature is 37°C. Just a degree or so above this, and you feel too hot; a degree or so below, and you feel too cold. When we are healthy, our bodies have ways of keeping our temperature from getting too hot or too cold.

How the blood controls warmth

Our blood flows all around our bodies, taking heat from hot muscles and sending it close to the skin, where it can cool by radiation and through contact with the air (conduction and convection). If we get too hot, more blood flows close to the skin. If we get cold, less blood flows near the skin.

Sweating

When water **EVAPORATES**, it takes heat from its surroundings. This works like a natural refrigerator and is used when the body gets very hot. People, and some other animals, lose water to keep cool—in this case it is called **SWEATING** (Picture 1).

▼(Picture 1) Sweat is made in special coiled tubes inside the skin. Sweat contains water and other substances that the body wants to remove. The sweat comes to the surface through an opening called a pore. The water evaporates, leaving the other substances on the surface of the skin.

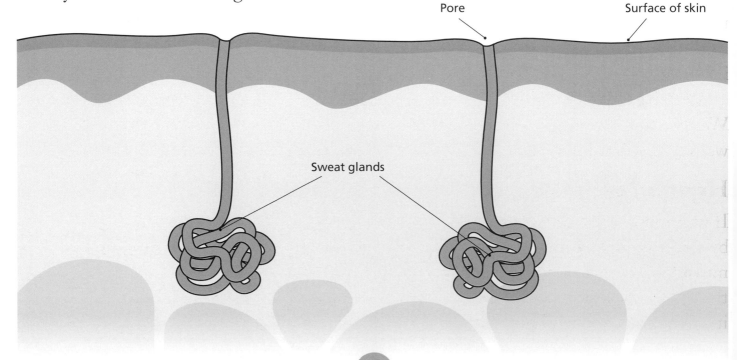

Pore

Surface of skin

Sweat glands

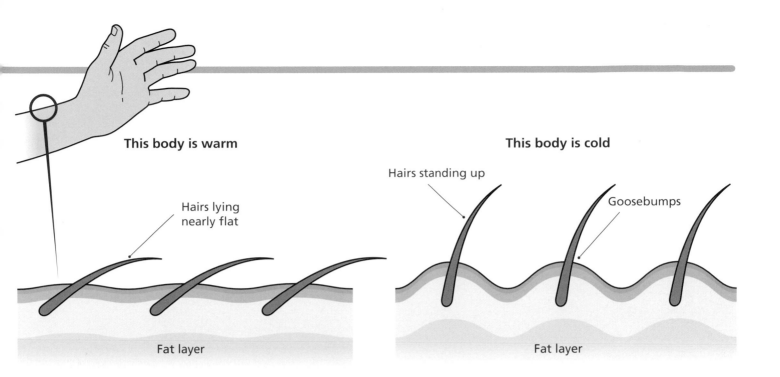

This body is warm

Hairs lying nearly flat

Fat layer

This body is cold

Hairs standing up

Goosebumps

Fat layer

▲ (Picture 2) Goosebumps, or goose pimples, are produced when the skin becomes cold. The muscles in the skin raise the hairs to trap more air. This also has the effect of producing goosebumps. Since we have fewer hairs than most furry animals, this is not an especially effective way of keeping warm. The fat layer below the skin does a much better job of insulating against the cold.

Shivering

We have a layer of fat below the skin. It acts like a natural insulator, keeping most of the body heat inside. When we get too cold, however, the body spots the danger signs, and the muscles in the skin start to raise the hairs, causing **GOOSEBUMPS** (Picture 2). At the same time, we start to shake violently. We call this uncontrollable shaking **SHIVERING**. Shivering makes the muscles work, and in doing so they release heat.

We have no control over shivering. We continue shivering until the body has warmed up above the danger level.

Hypothermia

If we cannot warm ourselves up enough by shivering, the body uses more extreme measures. The muscles stop shaking, and the body now tries to save what little heat it still has for as long as possible.

It shuts down all of the circulation to the skin and keeps warm blood flowing only to essential parts like the heart and brain. That is why people become very still when they are dangerously cold. But by shutting down like this, the body cannot continue for long; and without help a person in this state would die. Life-threatening coldness is called **HYPOTHERMIA**.

Summary
- Our bodies work well only in a narrow temperature range.
- The body can help keep its temperature steady by changing where blood flows.
- If the body gets too cold, there is a risk of death.

Using clothes to keep warm

To keep ourselves warm, we need to keep too much heat from leaving our bodies.

Keeping our bodies warm is vital, but we have to think about comfort and movement as well as warmth.

Warm clothing

The easiest way to keep warm is to keep cold air or water from moving past our bodies and carrying heat away by conduction.

One of the best insulators is **PLASTIC**. We could wrap ourselves in plastic sheet or plastic foam. That would keep us warm, but within a few seconds we would be very uncomfortable. That is because we are always losing moisture, as well as heat, through our skin in the form of sweat. Plastic will not allow moisture to go through it, and so the moisture trapped near our skin would soon make the plastic clammy and wet. Within a short time we would be so uncomfortable that we would be pulling the plastic off.

▼ (Picture 1) Our skin loses heat by conduction and radiation. Sweating also cools our skin. Clothes must keep in the heat but also let the skin lose moisture ("breathe").

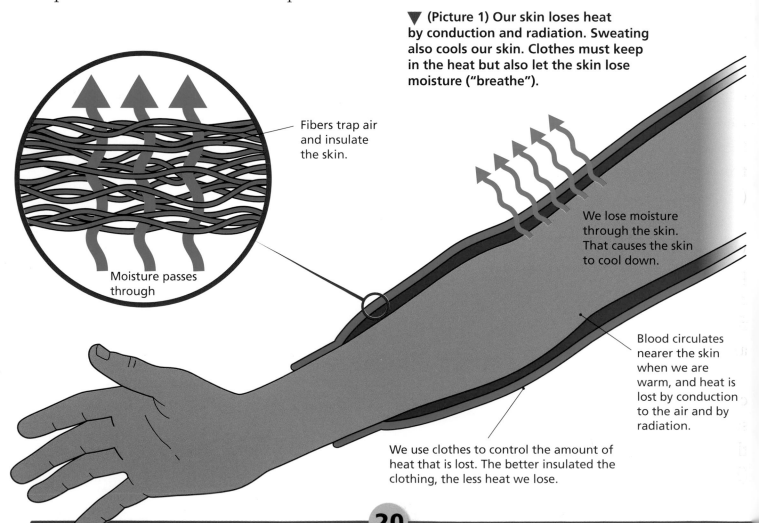

Fibers trap air and insulate the skin.

Moisture passes through

We lose moisture through the skin. That causes the skin to cool down.

Blood circulates nearer the skin when we are warm, and heat is lost by conduction to the air and by radiation.

We use clothes to control the amount of heat that is lost. The better insulated the clothing, the less heat we lose.

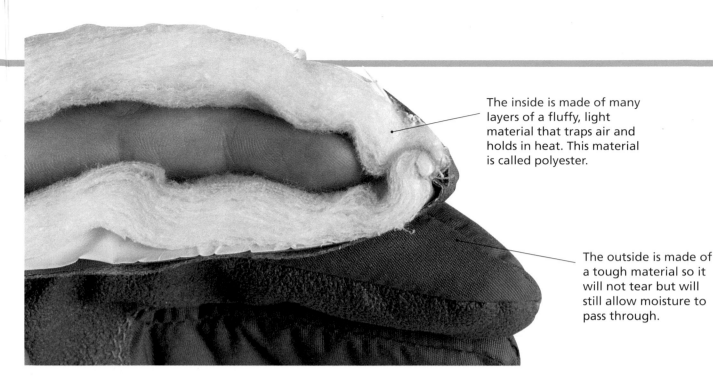

The inside is made of many layers of a fluffy, light material that traps air and holds in heat. This material is called polyester.

The outside is made of a tough material so it will not tear but will still allow moisture to pass through.

▲ (Picture 2) This cross section of a ski glove shows how many layers of fiber are used to trap air and insulate the fingers.

Letting clothing breathe

The secret to keeping warm and comfortable was discovered thousands of years ago. It was to wear clothes made of **FIBERS**. Materials made from fibers are not solid, but are thin strands that are **WOVEN** together into a fine net (Picture 1).

Curiously, when we use fibers, we are not really using the insulating property of the fiber. Instead, we are relying on trapping air between the fibers. Air is a very good insulator and also weighs very little.

If we trap air, we keep it from circulating and stop convection. At the same time, moisture can escape into the air, so we feel more comfortable (Picture 2).

Using the weave

We can trap different amounts of air, depending on the fiber we use and the way it is woven. Think about wool, for example. It is a naturally curly and bulky fiber, so it weaves together to make a cloth that traps lots of air and is naturally warm. It is good for when we need to be in places that are cold.

Now think about cotton. It is a naturally fine fiber that packs down well. As a result it does not hold as much heat as wool and is more suitable for use when we want to protect ourselves from the heat of the Sun as well as slight cool breezes. That is why it is used in many hot countries.

Summary
- Clothes prevent air moving over the skin and carrying heat away by conduction.
- Clothes trap insulating air between fibers.
- Fibers need to be woven in order to let moisture escape, as well as keep heat in.

How animals keep warm and cool

Animals have all of the problems that we have in keeping warm and cool. An animal's shape and how it behaves often give you a clue to how it keeps warm and cool.

Remaining at just the right temperature is as important for animals as it is for people. Here are two examples to show you how different animals keep warm.

Alligators and other reptiles

Reptiles include alligators, crocodiles, and lizards. They are **COLD-BLOODED** creatures, which means they use heat from their surroundings to keep warm.

At the same time, a reptile can only become active if its body is at a certain temperature. That is why all reptiles sunbathe in the first part of the day. By sunbathing, they soak up radiation from the Sun, and it heats up their blood so they can become more active. That is why you can spot reptiles on sunny stones, and why alligators come out of the water and sit on river banks (Picture 1). Once they are warm enough, they can begin to hunt for food.

Because it depends on heat from the Sun, a reptile will be much less active on a cold day than on a hot one.

A reptile loses heat through its mouth. That is why alligators, for example, often keep their mouths open (they gape). It keeps them from overheating.

Reptiles must be careful not to get too hot. Alligators, for example, cool off in the water.

▼ (Picture 1) Alligators sunbathe in the early part of the day to heat up their blood.

Elephants

Elephants are **WARM-BLOODED** creatures and can cool themselves using their blood supply in the same way human beings do. Most elephants live near the equator, where it is always hot, and so the main problem is how to keep cool.

Elephants can sweat; but then they lose a lot of water, and that can be a problem because elephants live in very dry parts of the world where water is not always easy to find. So instead of sweating, they keep cool by using their ears!

You may have noticed how when you are hot, your ears also become hot. Ears are very good at losing heat because they stand out in the air. They lose heat by conduction, convection, and radiation. Now look at an elephant's ears. Their massive size allows more blood to flow through them, so they lose heat very efficiently (Picture 2). By gently flapping them back and forth, an elephant also makes more air flow over them, increasing the amount of heat lost by conduction.

▲▼ (Picture 2) Elephants circulate their entire blood supply through their ears once every 2 minutes. They also spray themselves with water, and wallow in mud to cool down by evaporation.

Summary
- Animals have many different ways of keeping warm and cool.
- Cold-blooded animals, like alligators, use the Sun to warm up.
- Warm-blooded animals, like elephants, use conduction, convection, and radiation to cool down.

Index

Science Matters!

Grolier Educational

First published in the United States in 2003 by Grolier Educational, Sherman Turnpike, Danbury, CT 06816

Copyright © 2003
Atlantic Europe Publishing Company Ltd.

All rights reserved. No part of this publication may be reproduced, stored in a retrieval system, or transmitted in any form or by any means— electronic, mechanical, photocopying, recording, or otherwise—without prior permission of the publisher.

This product is manufactured from sustainable managed forests. For every tree cut down at least one more is planted.

Author
Brian Knapp, BSc, PhD

Educational Consultant
Peter Riley, BSc, C Biol, MI Biol, PGCE

Art Director
Duncan McCrae, BSc

Senior Designer
Adele Humphries, BA, PGCE

Editor
Lisa Magloff, BA

Illustrations
David Woodroffe

Designed and produced by
Earthscape Editions

Reproduced in Malaysia by
Global Color

Printed in Hong Kong by
Wing King Tong Company Ltd

Picture credits
All photographs are from the Earthscape Editions photolibrary.

Library of Congress Cataloging-in-Publication Data
Knapp, Dr. Brian J.
Science Matters! / [Dr. Brian J. Knapp].
p. cm.
Includes index.
Summary: Presents information on a wide variety of topics in basic biology, chemistry, and physics.
Contents: v. 1. Food, teeth, and eating—v. 2. Helping plants grow well—v. 3. Properties of materials—v. 4. Rocks and soils—v. 5. Springs and magnets—v. 6. Light and shadows—v. 7. Moving and growing—v. 8. Habitats—v. 9. Keeping warm and cool—v. 10. Solids and liquids—v. 11. Friction—v. 12. Simple electricity—v. 13. Keeping healthy—v. 14. Life cycles—v. 15. Gases around us—v. 16. Changing from solids to liquids to gases—v. 17. Earth and beyond—v. 18. Changing sounds—v. 19. Adapting and surviving—v. 20. Microbes—v. 21. Dissolving—v. 22. Changing materials—v. 23. Forces in action—v. 24. How we see things—v. 25. Changing circuits.
ISBN 0-7172-5834-3 (set)—ISBN 0-7172-5835-1 (v. 1)—ISBN 0-7172-5836-X (v. 2)—ISBN 0-7172-5837-8 (v. 3)—ISBN 0-7172-5838-6 (v. 4)—ISBN 0-7172-5839-4 (v. 5)—ISBN 0-7172-5840-8 (v. 6)—ISBN 0-7172-5841-6 (v. 7)—ISBN 0-7172-5842-4 (v. 8)—ISBN 0-7172-5843-2 (v. 9)—ISBN 0-7172-5844-0 (v. 10)—ISBN 0-7172-5845-9 (v. 11)—ISBN 0-7172-5846-7 (v. 12)—ISBN 0-7172-5847-5 (v. 13)—ISBN 0-7172-5848-3 (v. 14)—ISBN 0-7172-5849-1 (v. 15)—ISBN 0-7172-5850-5 (v. 16)—ISBN 0-7172-5851-3 (v. 17)—ISBN 0-7172-5852-1 (v. 18)—ISBN 0-7172-5853-X (v. 19)—ISBN 0-7172-5854-8 (v. 20)—ISBN 0-7172-5855-6 (v. 21)—ISBN 0-7172-5856-4 (v. 22)—ISBN 0-7172-5857-2 (v. 23)—ISBN 0-7172-5858-0 (v. 24)—ISBN 0-7172-5859-9 (v. 25)
1. Science—Juvenile literature. [1. Science.] I. Title.

Q163.K48 2002
500—dc21
2002017302